HOLY MOLÉ GUACAMOLE!

& OTHER TUMMY TALES

"Things changed like needles on a pine tree in spring. But the roots remained firmly planted in the rich dark earth. She was Diné. She had always been Diné, she always would. And as her tears fell, she remembered more than she knew."

Shari,
   We all have stories that we can tell about Eiber, but family stories are more important. Sit around a table of food and tell them.
   Enjoy my stories.

1

Carl

COLORADO COUNCIL
ON THE ARTS

This Covisions project is supported by a grant from Colorado Council on the Arts, a state agency funded by the Colorado General Assembly. Covisions is an annual program designed to support the creation and exhibition of innovative artist projects. For information about Covisions contact CCA Associate Director, Daniel Salazar at (303) 894-2619.

Editor: Jennifer Heath

Design: Karen Malzeke-McDonald

Printing: Quality Press, Denver, CO

Baskun Books-Boulder, CO
ISBN# 1-887997-07-5

HOLY MOLÉ GUACAMOLE!

& OTHER TUMMY TALES

BY ReNee FAJARDO
&
CARL RUBY

ILLUSTRATED BY
LOKKEN MILLIS

BASKUN BOOKS
BOULDER, CO

*Dedicated to the loving memory of my grandparents,
who helped make my dreams come true. To my family
and friends, who helped and supported me. And, of course,
to my children, the spices of my life.*
E. Renee Fajardo

*Dedicated to all the Colorado Rubys with mountains
of love and an avalanche of affection.*
Carl Ruby

*Dedicated to my mother Bonnie, who framed all my
pretty pictures when I was little.*
I love you!
Lokken Millis

TABLE OF CONTENTS

Holy Mole'! Guacamole!

The Real-life Antics of John Fajardo, 40 Years Ago,
When He Graduated from High School

by Renee Fajardo

John was a good boy. Everyone said so. Especially his Auntie Lucy, who doted on his every move. He was, after all, smart and handsome, and he could play the piano like an angel. Aunt Lucy thought he hung the moon above and threw in a few stars just for good measure. Soon, he would be off to college to study teaching, the first in his family.

John's great-grandparents had come from Delta, Colorado. They lived in an adobe ranch house that they built themselves and had worked the land much as their ancestors before them. They were farmers and ranchers and gatherers of herbs. No one had ever dreamed of going to college, until John. Aunt Lucy knew this feat deserved one of the best and biggest fiestas ever, and she planned to throw that party herself, complete with music and food.

Aunt Lucy invited all the aunts and uncles. She invited all the nieces and nephews and all the cousins and all the grandparents and the entire neighborhood to celebrate. No fiesta would compare to the one Auntie Lucy was going to have for John's high-school graduation. For a whole week before the party, Aunt Lucy and the other women shopped for food. There were pinatás to buy and fill with candy for the young ninos´, there were decorations to make, tablecloths to be ironed. The house was to be cleaned from top to bottom. The grass to be trimmed, the windows washed inside and out, the silver polished, the best china dusted. This was going to be a fiesta no one would ever forget.

On the day of the big event, Auntie Lucy and the others began cooking early. The steam from the pinto beans and the tamales fogged the windows. Pans of enchiladas were baked. Dozens of tortillas were patted out. Onions, tomatoes and chilies were chopped for salsa. Chicken was boiled for the molé and thick broths of green chili simmered on the stove. The smells from the house floated across the neighborhood. Everyone's mouth watered in anticipation of John's party. And John looked forward to this night with glee. In fact, he could hardly contain his laughter.

Because what Aunt Lucy forgot every time she bragged about how wonderful her nephew was — how smart and how handsome and how beautifully he played the piano — was that John was also ornery as the day was long!

She forgot the time John tied Uncle Avel's shoelaces together when he was sleeping on the couch. She forgot the time poor Uncle George, who had bad eyesight, brushed his teeth with hair cream instead of toothpaste. She forgot the time cousin Joanne reached into the bait box to grab a worm and grabbed a dead snake instead, and yelled so loud you could hear her clear across the lake. She forgot the time Aunt Mary looked for her false teeth all morning long, only to discover them in the bread box biting a piece of bread. She forgot the time cousin Napoleon was fed a liverwurst sandwich made out of canned dog food. Yes, Auntie Lucy forgot a lot of things. But John was young, and John was smart, and John did not forget.

He knew this party was a party of all parties and that not only must he come up with a good prank, he must out-prank himself. And he thought long and he thought hard, because he knew this couldn't be an ordinary prank, it must be something that nobody would ever forget. Nobody in the whole, entire fiesta could ever walk away and say they had not seen John's prank.

It couldn't be something like spiders in the ice cubes. Or whoopee cushions under the couch. It had to be something deliciously mischievous. And as he thought and thought, he smelled the chicken molé in the kitchen cooking. He considered how everybody always raved over Aunt Lucy's wonderful chicken molé. How delicate its flavor. How mild. How anyone could eat it, because it was easy on the palate. And then it hit John. That was it! He knew when it was time to eat, everyone would gather at the table and he would sit at the head of the table and they would wait for him to take the first bite of food. John knew what he was going to do. He would take a bite of Auntie Lucy's chicken molé first. And as he swallowed, he would pretend to choke and sputter. He would gag and turn around, and then he would faint. Everybody would stare at him in horror and rush over to him. He would rasp, "It's hot. It's so hot." And as they all gathered around him, clucking, "Oh, my, oh my! Aunt Lucy's chicken mole is too hot!" he would jump up and scream, "Holy Molé!" and begin to laugh and nobody would ever forget that prank.

The night of the big fiesta arrived and all the guests crowded into the small kitchen. John, the guest of honor, filled his plate first and went to sit at the head of the table where he waited in anticipation. After everyone else was seated, and Uncle Avel had made a toast and John's father had made a toast, and John's mother gave a toast, and his Auntie Lucy did, too, it was time to begin eating. John held up his bowl of chicken molé and was just about to take a big bite when cousin Joanne popped up from the other end of the table.

"Wait, John," she said. "Napoleon and I have a surprise for you."

With that, cousin Joanne went to the refrigerator and pulled out a small bowl of green goo. John looked. "Guacamole?"

"Yes," said cousin Joanne. "Napoleon and I saved all our allowance."

John was impressed. "Avocados are so expensive and so hard to find. I haven't had guacamole since last year. How nice of you."

Cousin Joanne shined him a big smile. "Oh, cousin John, you're so wonderful and we're all so very proud of you. Nothing is too expensive or too good for you." And with that, she handed the bowl of guacamole to John. He was so excited he forgot all about his prank. His tastebuds longed to savor the delicate mixture of garlic and herbs and the rich texture of avocados. He could hardly wait. He piled a huge, heaping tablespoon of the green heaven onto a tortilla. He popped the whole conglomeration into his mouth.

Something was wrong. Something was very, very wrong. The guacamole was not like any guacamole he had ever had in his whole life. It was extremely, exceedingly hot! His eyes began to tear and his ears began to burn. He could hardly stop himself from choking. But he could not sputter and spit the green droplets all over everybody at the table. There was nothing to do but swallow. So swallow he did. The longest, slowest, most agonizing swallow of his whole life. Beads of sweat gathered on his forehead. He gasped and cried out in a small voice, "Water, water."

Cousin Joanne began to laugh. "We'll get you water, cousin John."

Cousin Napoleon began to laugh. Everyone else looked on in horror. Uncle Avel said, "Joanne, you didn't use your grandma Lucy's recipe for guacamole, did you?"

Joanne laughed even louder. "I certainly did, Papa, and I followed it exactly like it said." Then she laughed some more.

John, meantime, was drinking glass after glass of water, sputtering and choking and turning red. Finally, he composed himself. He looked at the awestruck faces around the table and yelled, "Holy Molé! Guacamole! That's the hottest guacamole I've ever had in my whole life."

And with that, everybody burst into laughter and they laughed so hard tears came to their eyes. They laughed so hard, they almost fell off their chairs.

Even John laughed at himself.

"Okay," he said. "Let's eat!" And he took a great, big bite of Auntie Lucy's chicken molé and he did not say another word.

Holy Mole´! Guacamole!
Recipes by Lucy Lucero

3 large ripe avocados
1 tablespoon minced garlic
1/2 cup fresh chopped cilantro
1/2 cup diced tomatoes
2-4 diced jalapenos*
1 tablespoon fresh lime juice
1 teaspoon salt

Cut avocados in half. Take out seeds and scoop out meat with a spoon. Mash thoroughly with fork or potato masher. Put in lime juice. Stir. Then add remaining ingredients. Mix well. Serve with chips or as a garnish for tacos, burritos, taquitos, etc.   Makes approximately 2 cups.

*This recipe is very hot. You may decrease or delete the jalapenos.

Taquitos

1 dozen corn tortillas
2 boiled chicken breast
2 tablespoons chili powder
1/2 teaspoon cumin
1 teaspoon salt.
1/2 teaspoon garlic powder

Shred chicken breast. Mix chicken and spices together. Grease small frying pan with about a tablespoon of vegetable oil. Cook corn tortillas on both sides until soft, approximately 15 seconds on each side, more or less if needed.

Remove and place on a plate covered with a paper towel to drain. Transfer one tortilla at a time to a clean plate that you will use to assemble your taquito. Place approximately 2 tablespoons of the chicken mixture on one end of the tortilla evenly and roll up like a burrito. Deep fry in hot oil until crisp. Continue this process until all chicken is used.

Drain taquitos on paper towel.

Serve with dips such as salsa, guacamole and sour cream.

Soup's On!

The Ruby Family's New Year's Day Tradition

by Carl Ruby

Winter in Upstate New York.

Snow falls all day. The wind blows all night and blows the snow into drifts over six-feet tall. Damp cold. The thermometer stuck below freezing and no sun for months.

When I was a kid, I was too busy having fun to care. I sledded, built super snow caves and forts, sucked on yard-long icicles. After years of practice I could make the most heavenly snow angels, some on the steep side of drifts that looked like the angels were standing up! When the snow was just right for packing, I made snowmen of unusually large size. I found wooden boards and used them as ramps to roll the body parts and head into the correct positions. When my sled broke, a cardboard box became a toboggan. It was hard to find a dry pair of mittens.

Ma made a pot of soup every day. Chicken, beef, pork, barley, rice, noodle, vegetable, potato and even a pancake soup. The house was saturated with the warm smells of soup, a treat after a hard day of play. Pa had to have potatoes and meat at every dinner. Their aroma entwined with the scent of apple cake, apfel kuchen, for dessert.

We knew dinner would soon be served when Pa brought the milk up to the house for Ma to strain and pasteurize. He washed and took his usual chair at the head of the rectangular table in the dining room. I sat to his right and Ma on the left, closest to the kitchen.

My parents were Germans, who immigrated in 1929 and met in a night-school English class. Both became American citizens. After they married, they lived in Syracuse. When I was just finishing second grade at Garfield School, we moved to a small farm. Pa commuted to a regular city job, but he raised pigs, cows, steers, chickens, ducks, geese, rabbits and sometimes a goat. I helped with the livestock chores.

Pa named all the animals, but they were not just to keep and feed. My grandfather ran a butcher shop in Germany and Pa acquired his father's skills in slaughtering, meat-cutting and sausage-making. We never lacked for fresh meats, even if it was "Bessie" we were eating. Pa smoked ham and bacon in a small, unused milkhouse next to the barn.

The garden got bigger each year, and Ma canned and froze the vegetables we didn't eat fresh. Keeping the garden weed-free in those hot, humid summers was a formidable task. I helped to hill the potatoes and weed and thin the carrots and onions. The least favorite of my garden jobs was to pick the worms off the tomato plants. Pa just grabbed them with his bare hands. I preferred scraping those large, bright, green-horned monsters with a stick until they fell into a can. Despite the hard work, at harvest time, we all gladly ate the good food together.

My mother could transform any scraps into a culinary soup delight. Soup during those gloomy, chilly winters made each supper richer and healthier.

But each year, on December 31, it was Pa who ruled the kitchen — only he could make the New Year's lentil soup and only on that day. The smoked ham bone left over from Christmas dinner was the stock. The recipe was entirely in his head, memorized through generations of family tradition. There was some other custom, too, about pickled herring ... but all I remember was that wonderful soup. I sat in his chair at the dining room table and watched as he prepared the ingredients. He used the potatoes I had hilled, the carrots and onions I thinned and weeded.

One year, he made a huge milk pail full of lentil soup to take to a big community party. He smiled and hummed as he cooked. Once he wore Ma's flowered frilly apron. He looked funny, but I never told him. I wanted to get him a chef's hat for this occasion. It would have been a crowning touch, but I never did.

As he worked, he talked about his boyhood in the small German town of Offenbach am Glan and how the whole town

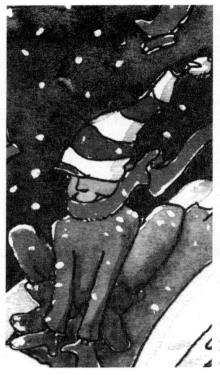

made lentil soup for New Year's. To eat the lentil soup first thing in the new year was said to bring prosperity and luck. He also talked about the year to come. Maybe we'd take a trip to Canada or buy a new, used tractor or build a corn crib. While Pa cooked, Ma darned socks in the living room. He loved this day and he loved to share the secret of the lentil soup. The tradition started right after the supper meal was eaten, as soon as the dishes were done.

On New Year's Eve 1969, Pa was dying. Ma invited a houseful of friends for a party and Pa knew this would be his last. He was cordial, but not talkative. Then he smelled that familiar aroma — the lentil soup. He lit up and came to life almost as he'd been before his illness.

It was I who'd made the lentil soup. I'd watched my father make that soup for so many years, I remembered how, and now, I could make it myself. As I handed Pa his bowl at the stroke of midnight, he looked up, his eyes glistening with tears. Then he grinned, content to know that his spirit would live on through the generations with the making of the soup each New Year's Eve. When he died in the spring, I understood that the magic of the soup had worked, for he left us quickly and painlessly, and we prospered with his memory.

Since then, I've made the lentil soup every New Year's. It transports me back home to upstate New York, to those harsh winters in a happy, soup-making home.

Pa's Lentil Soup

1 ham bone or several ham shanks
1 pound bag of lentils
6 to 8 cups water
1 teaspoon salt
1/2 teaspoon white pepper
3 to 4 potatoes
3 to 4 carrots
3 to 4 stalks of celery
1 onion (large)
1 tablespoon cooking oil
2 tablespoons flour with water (for thickening)

Wash and sort* the lentils in a sieve. Soak lentils in water for about one hour or until all ingredients are ready.

Wash, peel and cube potatoes in to1/4 inch to 1/2-inch size. Place in water. Drain before adding to soup.

Wash, peel and chop the carrots into 1/8" pieces.

Wash and chop the celery to the same size as the carrots.

Chop the onion coarsely and brown in a frying pan with the cooking oil. Set aside until soup is almost done.

Rinse the lentils again. Place them in a stock pot with 6 to 8 cups fresh water. Combine the ham bone, potatoes, carrots, celery, salt and pepper, and simmer for 1 to 2 hours, or until lentils are very tender. Stir occasionally.

Remove the ham bone and strip off the meat. Return the meat to the pot.

Add the browned onions.

Make a paste with the flour and water. Add to the soup until a desired consistency is achieved.

Serves 8 to 10 people (makes about 3 quarts)

*Lentils are a natural product, but despite the use of modern cleaning equipment, it is not always possible to remove all foreign materials.

Black-Eyed Pea Universe

Bob Hall Tells About the First Time He Saw a Bowl of Black-Eyed Peas

by Renee Fajardo

It was a beautiful New Year's day. Perhaps the most beautiful that Bob had seen in all his 16 years. The sun glowed golden yellow on the dead brown lawns. The blue sky was clear, with only an occasional wisp of snow-white cloud. The naked trees stretched their bony branches into the heavens.

Bob sighed as he ran the palm of his hand across the window pane. It made a horrendous, squeechy sound. The air outside was still cool and crisp, you could probably even see your breath if you were outside. But how would he know? He wasn't allowed outside until after dinner. By all rights, he should have been out two hours ago, gone down to Amese Park to shoot hoops with Ivan the Madman and James Tucker. But Mama didn't see it that way. The family would stay put until after New Year's dinner, period, end of story. It had been that way when their dad had been stationed in Germany. It had been that way when they lived in Italy and in California and it would be that way here in Colorado. Pop may have been the staff sergeant, but Mama was the general when it came to the family.

Mama's cooking made the windows steam up something fierce. Bob took the palm of his hand across the glass again. The noise was deafening. His brother, Ron, looked up from his Wall Street Journal in annoyance. "Look here, Spacehead, some of us would like to enjoy the peace and quiet of the holiday."

Bob rolled his eyes. What would a bookworm like his brother know about the lure of a heated game of basketball? The wind in your face, the sun in your eyes and sweat trickling down your forehead as the adrenaline pumped in your veins. There were only two years between Bob and Ron, but you would have thought it was more like a million.

"Bob! Time to set the table! Go get your sister," Mama called from the kitchen. Bob glared at Ron. Ron, of course, was immune from duty. He was reading!

Just then, Sherry walked into the living room. "Aw, come on, Bob, the window will still be there after dinner. Besides, you know Ron will have to clean up after." His sister was always so diplomatic. Bob followed her to the kitchen.

The smell of dinner danced across the room. A rich mixture of warm and familiar aromas. Bob instinctively knew what was on the stove and in the oven. These smells had been part of his mother's repertoire even before he was born. She had learned to cook when she was just a small girl in Kansas City. It didn't matter where in the world she was, the home cooking learned down by the banks of the Great Missouri was her legacy. There was something almost church-like about Mama's cooking. Like hearing your favorite gospel when you weren't really even listening for it. You weren't exactly surprised, just forgetful, about how much you liked it. You sort of opened your eyes real wide and sighed, "Oh, yeah!"

Bob's mouth watered. His stomach churned as he laid out the knives and forks.

"Oh, Gail, you can't be serious! Oh, girl, no one could have gotten away with that, only you, girl, only you!" His mother shrieked with laughter.

This was followed by more hysterics. Bob was mortified. His mother was on the phone with Aunt Gail, the family gossip and there was no telling what wild tale she was telling, nor how long the rendition would last. This was a sure sign dinner would be delayed while Mama called everyone else in her family to recount Aunt Gail's story. Sure enough, a few minutes later, his mom was saying, "Happy New Year, Sister Syble." This was followed by more gibbering, followed by greetings to Grandma Rena and Uncle Conrad. Then came Cousin Nita and Therman, Jr.

Bob thought more and more about food and less and less about basketball. Then, to his relief, his mother hung up the phone. Dinner was on the way.

"Brinnng!!! Brinnng!!!" The phone rang again.

"Hello ... ooooh, my, what a nice surprise. Happy New Year to you, too," Mama cooed. "Honey, it's your brother and family in Pennsylvania!"

This was all he needed! Now his dad would be on the phone forever. Bob tried to drown out the conversation. Hi, how are you? How is uncle so and so? How is sister Naomi? How are brother Rudy and niece Lucille? Would it never end? Finally, Bob heard his father hang up the phone. He looked outside to see if the tulips had come up. Mama called, "Dinner's ready!" Music to his ears at last.

They all sat down at the table and said grace. Bob's tastebuds stood at attention. Food, glorious food. Hallelujah! First came the succulent, honey-baked ham, glazed with tropical pineapple slices. Next, his sister passed the golden, steamy corn bread that Mama always put just a wee bit too much sugar in. Bob put a huge pat of butter on it and watched the creamy delight ooze down the sides of the bread. Next came the Southern-fried chicken. The crispy crunch of the crust could be heard all the way back to Missouri. Hmmm. Good.

Next came a big bowl of mashed potatoes and gravy just begging to be plopped onto his plate. Then garden-fresh green beans steamed to perfection. This was bliss. The world was perfect. Nothing could ruin this glimpse of sensory ecstasy. Nothing!

From somewhere at the outer limits of the table, a bowl was passed. It came a few seconds after Bob had helped himself to a generous portion of his mother's famous greens, so he was not expecting anything upsetting. Bob's wrist made the flicking, scooping movement into the bowl. What he pulled back was not only unexpected, but horrifying.

"Ugh!" Bob screamed in disgust and terror. He threw the

offending mass of glop back in the bowl.

His mother eyed him with disapproval. "After all these years, you think you'd learn how to act at the dinner table," she scolded, then she tried coaxing. "Just try them, Bob, you really will like them."

Bob stared at the bowl. He shuddered and cringed. They were staring back at him! Hundreds of piercing, little black eyes! How could he swallow something that was watching him as he ate them?

"I'm allergic to them," he stammered. One glance at his mother told him this was not being taken as a serious medical consideration. "And besides, I'm going to play ball with the guys later. If I eat much more, I'll get cramps."

That one worked. He was off the hook. Everyone stopped staring at him and resumed talking. His brother grabbed the bowl from him and served himself a big helping of the black-eyed peas. Bob winced. How could anyone eat all those beady eye-balls?

When the meal was finished, and the dishes were done, it was basketball time. Hallelujah! Bob's lanky, long body ran out the front door and all visions of those black-eyed peas from Mars vanished. The rhythm of the basketball was constant and reassuring. It was a clear, crisp day, and oh, so peaceful. Before he knew it he was at the park dribbling away to his heart's content. Nothing out of the ordinary—just a boy and his ball and his buddies.

Then, from almost mid-court, Bob sunk a basket.

Ivan the Madman's mouth fell open. Bob tripped over his shoes in awe. "What the heck was that? You eat spinach or something for dinner?" James Tucker said.

"Never seen the likes of that before except on TV," Ivan mused.

Bob looked sheepish and felt his face go red. "I don't know what you call that."

"I call it a three-pointer. That's what I call it. Too bad some of the other guys aren't around to see it," James Tucker lamented. "They wouldn't believe it!"

"Let's play." Bob was growing more uncomfortable by the minute.

Not that he didn't think the shoot was something special. It was just that he wasn't quite sure how it happened. Maybe things weren't always as they seemed. Maybe we just assume that everything is always going to be one way and can't be another way, then out of nowhere you find out it's possible for it to be different. Maybe that was what made life exciting and special. Maybe knowing there was always so much we hadn't seen or heard or done or tasted before was what kept human beings looking forward to each new day. Maybe every time you did something you'd done a million times before, it was still different from all those other times. Just like this game of basketball was different from the one he played yesterday. Maybe we shouldn't ever assume that something is going to be just one way until we go out and do it.

When Bob got home that night, he opened the refrigerator and put a big, heaping ladle of black-eyed peas into a sauce pan. He heated the contents on the stove. He poured the peas into a cereal bowl and sat down at the table. He stared bravely at all those beady little eyes and took a big bite. Then he took another bite and another bite and another.

"Lord have mercy, son! What's that all about?" His mother was astonished. "After sixteen years, you think you know your own boy, and the next minute he's eating black-eyed peas!"

Bob grinned. "It's a miracle, Mom. They are delicious. These black-eyed peas better watch out for my eyes and mouth and stomach. Yum!"

Black-Eyed Peas
Recipe by Bob Hall

6 cups or 2 bags black-eyed peas
8 cups water
1/2 teaspoon salt
1/2 teaspoon pepper
1 bulb garlic
1 onion, yellow or white
1 smoked turkey leg

Wash peas thoroughly, combine all ingredients in a large pot. Boil combined ingredients for 2 1/2 to 3 hours or until peas are soft, but not mushy. Keep an eye on the water level and add more if needed.

Serve over rice or enjoy with your favorite cornbread recipe.

Serves 4 to 6.

Eye-Opening Corn Bread
Recipe by Frank Trujillo

1 1/2 cups corn meal
1/2 cup all-purpose flour
1 1/2 cups milk with one tablespoon vinegar
1 tablespoon sugar
1 teaspoon salt
2 teaspoons baking powder
1/2 teaspoon baking soda
2 eggs
3 tablespoons chopped green onion
1/4 cup fresh chopped jalapenos or 2 tablespoons dried crushed red pepper

Preheat oven to 450°F

Combine all ingredients.

Pour into well-greased pan 8x8x2 inches. (You may use any other similar sized pan or pour into muffin cups).

Bake 25 to 30 minutes until golden.

Serves 6 to 8

Through Loving Eyes

*Twelve-year-old Kathy Girardo and her 65-year-old
Grandmother Girardo Tell the Story of the Italian Pizzelles
Hidden in the Cupboard*

by Carl Ruby

Kathy's Eyes:

Visiting Grandma is exciting. It means we're going to have another great adventure into THE PANTRY!

Grandma is my father's mother. Her real name is Josephine Girardo. Her parents and her older brothers and sisters came to America from Italy, but she was born in the United States, so she calls herself an American-Italian.

She's a great talker with words and hands. She laughs a lot. She has a sweet tooth and can beat me at jacks. And she always has a hug for each of my brothers and sisters and me. I like the way she takes my chin in her soft hands and gently lifts it up so I can see her sparkling eyes and smiling mouth. We love her.

Grandma lives in Boulder. We all pile into the Ford station wagon, a red one with the shiny dipping line on the side. As the Flatirons come into view, I know we're all thinking about the pantry.

We enter through the back of the house, where there's a covered screen porch and a Maytag ringer washing machine next to the doorway. It looks really OLD. Mother shakes her head.

Grandma greets us at the door. Homemade spaghetti simmers on the stove. The kitchen is large and well-lighted, with the usual kitchen stuff ... only older. There's a door with a crystal knob just to the side of stove. That's the entrance to the pantry.

The pantry is this place that looks like a small room, with no windows, like a walk-in closet with built-in shelves. The shelves hold Grandma's pots and pans, dishes, platters, uncooked foods, canned foods, pasta and our favorite thing, COOKIES! Grandma makes great cookies from oatmeal to chocolate chip to our favorite, the round, flat waffle cookie called pizzelles. Grandma says they're Italian. We know they're delicious! And the pantry is where they're hiding, just waiting for us.

Getting all six of us kids into the pantry without being seen is really easy. The grown ups eat the big meal in the dining room and we eat in the kitchen around the oval table. So when the adults finish eating, they start talking louder. Louder talking usually means no one will come into the kitchen for more food. That's our chance to slip into the pantry.

Keeping everyone quiet is the hard part. It's dark inside when the pantry door is closed. I can't quite reach the pull-string light. The only light is a line coming in from the bottom of the door. It gives the pantry a scary, spooky, haunted-house feeling.

"Be brave, Richard," I reassure my younger brother. "You know what we're here for."

Grandma is short and she keeps her cookies in pots on the top shelf. I don't know how she gets them up there. Being the oldest, I climb the lower shelves like a ladder to reach the top cookie shelf. It takes great skill to keep your balance and not make noise with the lids. It's dark, but by the time I make the climb, I can see the pots. Sometimes, I get lucky and there are cookies in the first pot. I set the pot's lid on another pot. I reach into the cookie jar with one hand and hold the shelf with the other so I won't fall. Then I climb down very quietly and hand out cookies.

The lid has to be replaced on the cookie jar pot or Grandma will know we were in there. So I have to climb the shelf ladder again. Sometimes I look into the other pots, hoping to find the pizzelles, but cookies are cookies.

Our exit is quick and easy. Closing the door quietly is a problem, because the crystal knob is slippery. Still, no matter how often we make the adventure into the pantry, we never get caught. I doubt to this day that Grandma knows we were in the pantry eating her cookies. We fool Grandma every time.

I'll tell her when I get older.

Grandma's Eyes:

Spaghetti's the best idea when the whole family comes for

Sunday afternoon dinner. I have enough tomatoes for a wonderful sauce. Those six kids will eat a potful and splatter most of it all over themselves. They like eating alone in the kitchen. They're real noisy at the start, but as they fill up, you wouldn't know they are there.

First, I better wash out my Sunday dress. The flowers go well with my black-gray hair. I still like to use that old ringer washer. It gets things clean without a lot of soap and water. The ringers squeeze out just enough moisture so the clothes dry fast on the porch line. My daughter-in-law wants me to get a more modern wash machine. I can tell by the way she shakes her head every time she sees the old Maytag.

Now to get the pizzelle iron. That iron came over on the boat with my family when they left Italy. It was one of the few things they brought with them. The iron has been in our family for as long as I can remember. My mother, bless her heart, gave it to me a long time ago. She said it is a piece of the old country I should never forget. It's hanging on a hook in the pantry.

Thank goodness for that small room. It's right handy by the stove. The doorknob is hard to turn, because it's a little greasy from all the cooking on the stove. But that pantry, with strong, built-in shelves around all the walls, holds all my pots and pans, dishes, large serving platters, pasta, uncooked and canned foods, and is the place I keep my favorite sweet-tooth things -- COOKIES.

Usually, I make the pizzelles for special occasions like Christmas and Easter. Kneading all the ingredients is getting to be a hard, tiring job. All those eggs to beat. One day, maybe, I should get an electric mixer! I enjoy rolling the dough into walnut-sized balls. The waxed paper keeps them from sticking to the table.

Time to heat up both sides of the iron on the front gas burner. The black, cast- iron form is quick to heat up. A lick of my finger and a quick touch of the iron tells me it is hot and ready. I open it by the long handles and put in a ball of dough. When I close it, the dough squeezes flat. I put the iron back on the burner for about half a minute, then flip it over to cook the other side. When they're nicely brown, I take them off the heat and put them on to the oval table. The designs on the pizzelles are most interesting. The prettier side has six graceful flower-like petals. The other side is dotted with small squares and a tiny daisy in the center.

What's really interesting is the eating.

It takes a long time to make a whole batch, so I better place them out of my sight and the children's. I hide them in one of the big pots on the top shelf. I use the stepping stool behind the pantry door. I'm not too tall.

Last year, at the end of one of our Sunday afternoon meals, I went into the kitchen but the children weren't there. I thought they'd gone out on the porch to play. The next day, I noticed that the lid to my pizzelle pot was off and many cookies were missing. My sweet tooth isn't that bad! Did I forget to replace the lid? It happened again after the next family visit. I sprinkled a little flour on the floor of the pantry to see if mice were eating my cookies. What I found were six pairs of shoe prints all over the room. I don't know how the children get up to the top shelf for those cookies. The pantry is dark, with no windows. The light string is pretty high. I would think young Richard would be frightened of the dark. They go in there every time they visit. Now I can usually hear the door closing when they leave. They even nibble on my oatmeal and chocolate chip cookies.

"Anybody want more spaghetti?" I say rather loudly before I enter the kitchen.

I find the children sitting at the table with their heads hanging slightly down. I go to each and raise their heads by the chin. I like to look into their sparkling eyes. They smile and I brush the stray cookie crumbs from their lips. They think I don't know.

I'll tell them when they get older.

Italian Pizzelles

Note: The old-fashioned pizzelle irons have been modernized into electric ones. Electric mixers and irons make the preparation easier, so we can now enjoy pizzelles any time of the year. This recipe is for use with an electric pizzelle maker.

Pre-heat pizzelle maker

3 eggs, beaten

3/4 cup sugar

3/4 cup butter or margarine, melted

1 cup flour (less for thinner pizzelles)

1 teaspoon baking powder

3 teaspoons anise extract

1 teaspoon vanilla

Add and beat all ingredients in the order listed. Batter should be thick, yet flow from a spoon. Place about a tablespoon of batter in the center of each section on the electric pizzelle maker. Close lid. Cook until steaming stops, about 45-60 seconds. Remove with a fork. Cool on a wire rack or towels. Before eating, the pizzelles may be dusted with confectioners' sugar.

Makes 24 pizzelles.

Esther and the Tortillas

Ten-year-old Esther Lopez-Dussart Overcomes the Difficulties Encountered When Cultures Clash

by Renee Fajardo

Esther loved the smell of warm tortillas and how their smooth texture felt against her skin. She watched a square of butter melt into liquid glaze across the one she was about to devour. In the background, she could hear Mama patting a small ball of dough into another tortilla. The rhythm of the pat-pat-pat was like a lullaby. She could remember how her grandmother said that the tortilla had been a part of their family for generations, that the Lopez women had been making tortillas long before there were Lopezes, long before they had any white blood mixed with their Indian blood, long before they spoke English.

Esther's friends were waiting outside for her. Today, they were all going to the depot to throw rocks at the trains and maybe get the attention of the caboose man. After that, they would go skating in town, if Esther could find the skate key. She heard them yell, "Come on, Esther! The train's coming!" She tried to stuff the whole tortilla in her mouth. Her cheeks puffed like a chipmunk. She was not allowed outdoors with the tortillas, especially when other people were around.

Papa worked in the sugar mill in Eaton. That was the only place in town a man could find work if he wasn't a farmer or a railroad man. The family had moved here from the coal mine town of Summerset, when the mines closed down. Esther missed the cool mountain air and the life they'd left behind, but they had to make a living and the flat plains of Eaton were where that living

could be made. Unfortunately, Papa had changed more than jobs when they came here. He changed. His whole personality was different. He no longer had friends over to party and fiddle into the wee hours of the night. There was no longer storytelling around the kitchen table, where the soup bowls had endless bottoms. Papa's throaty laughter and merry smile no longer filled the ears of his children. The jovial, happy man they was knew was now a silent, brooding loner.

Papa was from Belgium and had come to America with his parents to make his fortune. Esther's mother was a beautiful Mexican woman and just the remedy for the harsh life of a miner. When he married Mama , he hadn't thought much about her being Mexican. In the 1920s, being of mixed blood was not a problem in Colorado mining towns. Everyone was from some different place. When people were inside the dangerous coal mines, it didn't matter what color they were. Everyone worked together to make sure they came out alive. They had to be just like a family. Therefore, folks in Summerset focused on the work, not the color of your hair. Up there they even had big doings where everyone brought the food they loved best. Mama brought tortillas and beans, Mrs. Pawloski brought kielbasa sausage, Mrs. Ginther brought sweet, red cabbage and Mrs. Martinez brought tripe soup. It was like an international bazaar right in the middle of town.

When they moved to Eaton, the parties stopped. Papa wouldn't allow the children to eat tortillas outside for fear people would realize they were part Mexican.

The children called again. They were going to leave without her. Esther grabbed a small stack of tortillas and hid them in her coat. They made her feel so warm. She could see her grandmother's long, black hair pulled back into a braid. She could hear the words the old woman always chanted, "por los ninos," over and over again as she patted out the little balls of dough. She could even smell the mesquite burning in the open fire that her grandmother had cooked over. The warm tortillas felt the same to Esther as they had felt to her grandmother, and to her grandmother before that and the grandmother before that. Flour now replaced ground maize, but the rest was the same. The wind still blew wildly across the Sangre de Cristo mountain range. The snow still blanketed the Earth in crystal silence. The Spring still smelled of moist tender greens. The summer sun still beat so hard upon the open fields of Eaton you could hear the ground crack. It was all still the same.

Esther ran out the door to join her friends. She unzipped her coat. She pulled out the fresh tortillas and offered them to the waiting children. The steam rose like prayers to heaven.

Tortillas
Recipes by Maria Ribera

2 cups all-purpose flour
1/4 teaspoon salt
2 teaspoons baking powder
1 teaspoon shortening or vegetable oil
1 cup lukewarm water

Mix all dry ingredients. Make a whole in the middle. Add shortening and water. Knead with your hands until all the shortening is blended with the flour mixture.

Knead the rest of the ingredients. Add more water or flour if needed, small amounts at a time, enough to make a soft, workable ball of dough.

Make small balls and roll out thin.

Cook over a hot griddle on both sides until the tortilla forms small bubbles and is lightly brown on top. Flip over and do the same for the other side until the dough is cooked.

Keep hot, wrapped in a towel, until ready to eat.

Serve with butter, jelly, or with dinner as a bread, or just by themselves.

Makes 1/2 dozen.

Salsa

1 29-ounce can whole, peeled tomatoes
2-3 jalapeno chilis (more for a hotter salsa)
1 small onion
3 big teeth of garlic (more can be added if desired)
1/2 cup fresh cilantro
1 teaspoon salt
1/2 teaspoon black pepper

In a large bowl, crush the tomatoes well with the juice. Set aside.

Dice onions as small as you can. Put into tomatoes. Stir.

Cut jalapenos as small as you can, start with two, because more can be added later if hotter salsa is preferred. Put into tomato and onion mixture. Stir.

Mince garlic and add to mixture and stir well. Add salt and pepper. Stir.

Pour into a clean container and refrigerate.

Serve with tortilla chips, over eggs, tacos, burritos, etc.

Makes 4 cups.

Christmas Dinner Down Under

Ian McMillan Recalls his 1966 Christmas Misadventures When He Was 14 Years Old.

by Carl Ruby

Everyone in Adelaide, South Australia, looked forward to Christmas. Mum had decorated our house and the gifts were ready to open. My sister, Jill, was anticipating a banner year for gifts. I, too, was hoping for more toys, especially model car kits.

My dad works for General Motors on the production line as a time-study analyst. He makes sure everything runs smoothly and in as little time as necessary. Our Christmas holiday is run in a similar manner, with not a wasted minute.

Bright and early at 7 o'clock on Christmas Day, we are up and opening the household Christmas gifts. We each received exactly the same number. Mum and Dad exchanged their usual husband-wife gifts: A white shirt and fancy tie for Dad and a ruffled blouse and silver necklace for Mum. Jill received some clothes and a beautiful doll. Wow! She liked that gift.

And me? Well, my gifts were nice, if you like shirts, pants, socks and underwear. Not a single toy. Not one model car kit. Nothing but clothes. This was not a good start to Christmas Day.

At precisely 8 o'clock, the children of our block on Attunga Street walked to Mr. Bucton's house for the traditional kids'

41

Christmas breakfast. Glasses of orange juice stood by empty plates, soon to be filled with Mr. Bucton's small egg pancakes. I enjoyed them, because he puts honey in the batter. We squeezed fresh lemon on the pancakes and then sprinkled them with granulated sugar.

The breakfast was okay, had it not been for the silly tradition that all of us kids were to compare our Christmas presents. Then we played with the other kids' stuff. Jill was excited about her doll and had a wonderful time. But who wants to compare and play with socks and underwear?

By 9 o'clock, we were on our way back to our house to get ready for the big midday feast. My father's family takes turns hosting the lunch. This year, we were going to Grandfather's. When Jill and I rounded the back of our house, we saw a terrifying sight.

Mum was hanging over the white picket back fence and she seemed to be crying hysterically. This scared me! When we got closer, we saw she laughing uncontrollably. Tears running down both cheeks. Was the stress of the holiday season too much for her? Breathlessly, she told us that she had just "pee'd" on the kitchen floor. Why was that so funny? I quickly ran into the kitchen and looked. There in the middle of the floor were the small, round green peas for our Christmas lunch. Mum had accidentally dumped them as she was shelling them. Mum had given me a fright, and so early in the Christmas day.

After calming Mum down, we helped her pick up the peas. Jill and I got dressed in our new clothes. Of course, everything I wore was new, except my shoes! All the food and gifts were loaded into the car and as the clock ticked toward 10, we arrived at Grandfather's.

How my mouth watered for Grandmum's roast turkey stuffed with bread and herb dressing. She cooks the turkey with potatoes, carrots and parsnips. She also makes ham and pickled pork. But as we sat down to eat at noon, Grandmum made a

shocking discovery: She had forgotten to turn on the oven. Cold, uncooked turkey! What else could go wrong?

The oven was turned on. The turkey started cooking. We all knew that by 4 p.m., we'd be going to Mum's folks and we usually took the leftovers from lunch to eat as the evening meal. Thank goodness for the ham.

For dessert, there is always a steamed plum pudding with hot custard. Grandmum's recipe is the greatest, because inside the pudding she mixes three pence and six pence coins. I was hoping to get a few, for that meant good luck – something I needed right now! It also meant that I could add them to my savings for a model car kit. But the way the day had already gone, I figured I'd better be careful not to chew down hard on a coin and chip a tooth and end up at the dentist's office.

No one found any coins in the pudding. Did Grandmum forget again? No. This year Australian money changed from the British Imperial form to the new Australian decimal coins and bills. Grandmum had heard that the new coins were not suitable for cooking.

Oh well. The pudding was delicious.

The trip to Mum's parents was uneventful. I wondered what more could go astray. We might have a car breakdown, but Dad always drives a GM vehicle. We arrived at 4 o'clock, right on schedule.

There was another gift exchange before we sat down to eat. Maybe this one would produce more than clothes. There's a limit to the number of socks and underwear a young lad should receive.

Wow! All the packages I opened contained toys. And three model car kits.

Things were looking up. The roast turkey, potatoes, carrots and parsnips were cooked to perfection. For dessert there was yellow layer cake with chocolate frosting and a cherry on every slice. My favorite. At 8 o'clock, our usual departure time, I didn't want to leave.

And we didn't.

With all the excitement of Christmas day, my father, the time-study control expert, forgot to wind his watch.

Mr. Bucton's Christmas Pancakes

1 cup flour
2 tablespoons sugar
1 tablespoon honey
3/4 cup milk
1 egg
pinch of salt.

Mix all ingredients to form a smooth batter. Drop on a hot griddle using a tablespoon. Pancakes will be flat and 2 to 3 inches across. Brown on both sides. Makes 15-18 small pancakes.

Serve with lemon juice and granulated sugar or with butter and jam or syrup.

ALFONSO'S BIRTHDAY SQUID

Twelve-year-old Asia Wright Tells the Story of Her Great-Grandfather Alfonso Fajardo's Immigration to the United States

by Renee Fajardo

I have five sisters and one brother. My family is very interesting. I think this is because my ancestors were so interesting.

Take, for instance, my great-grandpa, Alfonso. He was born in 1907 in Tarlac, Philippines. He spent his childhood swimming in the ocean and climbing palm trees to throw down coconuts to his cousins. He said they used to tease all the girls by chasing them around with creepy things they found washed up on the shore. I think that's where my little sister, Avalon, inherited her sense of humor.

In 1923, my great-Grandpa was hired as a deck hand on a ship headed for America. It went to China first and took six months before it got to California. My great-Grandpa said it was a very long trip! He didn't make much money and had to sleep on a little cot way in the bottom of the ship. A lot of people got really sick and said they never wanted to see the ocean again, but not my great-Grandpa! He said he always loved the sea, because it was the soup of life. I thought that was funny, but I think he was right.

When my great-Grandpa finally made it to California, he

was in the wrong city. He docked in San Francisco and was supposed to be 500 miles south in Los Angeles. His cousin, Jamie, and some other Filipino friends lived in Los Angeles and they were going to help him find a job and get his citizenship. They also could speak English fluently, which would be a big help since my great-Grandpa could only speak a few words of English. He knew how to say "where is" really good. After that, he would look in his dictionary and find the word he wanted to fill in the blanks. This worked out pretty well for the most part. He never had trouble finding the bathroom or a place to eat. These two things are very important when you are in a strange land, my great-Grandpa said. They are two things you have to do everyday and, unlike sleeping (which you have to do everyday, too), it's better not to do them in dark alleys or under park benches.

      Unfortunately, my great-Grandpa couldn't find the word "bus" in his dictionary. This may not seem like a big deal unless you are trying to figure out how to get from San Francisco to Los Angeles using the least amount of money possible. What my great-Grandpa did find in his dictionary was the word "taxi," which in Filipino translates as public transportation. So off he went, 500 miles in a taxi cab with a big self-satisfied grin on his face. He had figured out the American mass transit system, and, boy, it was swell — just him and the cabbie. When he arrived in Los Angeles, the cabbie had a big grin on his face. The fare was $75, which was equivalent to several hundred dollars today. My great-Grandpa was left with a total of thirty-five cents in his pocket!

      Somehow, things seemed to work out all right. My great-Grandpa ended up getting a job and his citizenship. Eventually, he moved to Denver, Colorado with his friends, where he met my great-Grandma. He worked as a waiter in a fancy lunch place called the Denver Tea Room. I guess back then eating lunch was a big deal, because there was real gold silverware on the table and white linen tablecloths. Everyone ate off porcelain plates and drank from real crystal glasses. My great-Grandpa had to wear a white jacket and dress pants when he worked. He said that people just loved to feel like they were eating in luxury sometimes, because it made them feel good to be treated special. Ordinary folks and famous folks could all eat together at the tea room and be treated equal. Sharing a fine dining experience was like everyone going to the same church. Everyone was polite, kind and peaceful for the hour they were there.

Eventually, my great-Grandpa and my great-Grandma had a baby boy, my grandpa John. That baby grew up, got married and had my Mom and my uncles. Then, my Mom grew up and had me, my five sisters and my brother. It's amazing how one little boat trip from the Philippines carrying my great-Grandpa led to all these people living here in Colorado. My great-Grandpa said life was funny in the way one little apple seed can turn into a whole orchard.

When my great-Grandpa was turning 84 years old, he wanted to have his orchard at his birthday party. He knew he was going to die pretty soon. It was important to him to have all the family there. All the grandchildren, great-grandchildren, aunts, uncles, his son and his daughter came. Special Filipino dishes were prepared for my great-Grandpa. It was the best way everyone knew to tell him how much they loved him. There was steamed rice, of course, chicken adobo (a rich chicken soup with vinegar and bay leaves), little eggrolls called lumpia, bean threads with pork, little plates of hot pepper in soy sauce, collard and mustard greens steamed in vinegar water, sweet rice, coconut pudding and something squishy and purple that my Aunt Coring from California made. My great-Grandpa was very, very happy when he saw it brought to the table. Not only was it weird and purple, it smelled bad, too! The rest of us had to hold our noses.

My great-Grandpa just laughed when he saw our faces. In his heavily accented, broken English, he said, "Here bee bees, it's very good!"

Then, he put a small glob of multi-armed creature on our plates. My sisters stuck their fingers in the weird purple sauce and finger-painted their napkins. "It's squid," my great-Grandpa laughed.

My brother dangled one of the tentacles off of his nose. "Why is it purple, old pa?" he asked.

"Because," snapped my sister Kali, "it's the ink. They use it as a smoke screen in the ocean."

With that, everyone's stomach turned. Great-Grandpa didn't seem to notice and went about enjoying his meal. Needless to say, not very many people ate their squids. A big bowl was left afterward.

Everyone was supposed to help clean up the table. The first set of twins, Tim and Syd, were only five, so they did the easy stuff like putting the leftovers in plastic containers. The second set of twins was too tiny to do anything. My great-Grandma saved every single cottage-cheese tub she had ever used. There was a whole shelf in the basement dedicated to cottage-cheese containers. Tim had the job of preserving the squid and ink sauce. I guess he thought the squid was too extraordinary for a plain old cottage-cheese tub, so he put it in a fancy jelly jar made of glass. It looked really pretty in there, too. No one would ever have guessed at the foul smelling slime it contained.

Later that night, after all the work had been done, and everyone had gone home, my great-Grandpa was relaxing on the couch watching the news. All of us great-grandchildren were playing in the big bedroom. We got to spend the night, which was always an adventure. My great-grandparents lived in a big, old, three-story Victorian house. It was full of antiques and old magazines. We always looked for hidden staircases, lost treasure and lonely ghosts. Great-Grandpa occasionally hid coins in cob-webbed corners for us to find. This made the little kids squeak like piglets. They got so excited, Kali and I had to cover our ears in order not to go deaf.

About 8 o'clock, great-Grandma yelled at one of us to go "draw a bath." That was an old-fashioned term for "fill up the tub." Avalon, my middle sister, who is a naturally mischievous person, volunteered for the job. Being seven, we understand she still thinks it's fun to put bells on the cat's tail or bring in disgusting little bugs from the garden. She cut the twins' hair the week before. Boy, was Mom mad! Sometimes, she is just plain nice. She'll give us licks on her popsicles or shares her candy with us. So, we thought she was being helpful when she volunteered to make a bubble bath.

Great-Grandma, who used to be a fun kid herself, knew how much everyone loved a good bubble bath. She even told Avalon she could use the lavender lilac stuff that was in the fancy jar. Great-Grandma would help Avalon start the water and pour the beautiful purple soap into the tub. She then left Avalon in charge of watching the level of bubbles. When they reached above the tub level, great-Grandma would give all the little ones a bath. "Piece of cake," Avalon said with a grin.

Five minutes later, Avalon called out, "Bubble alert!"

Great-Grandma called the little ones into the bathroom and told them to undress. "My, my, Avalon," great-Grandma said. "There sure are a lot of bubbles this time and the water is pretty purple. Did you use more bubble bath?"

Avalon looked down at the empty glass jar. So did great-Grandma. "Oh well. I guess it's all in fun, Avie." Great-Grandma said as she twitched Avalon's nose.

Avalon sat on the toilet as the four little ones (the double set of twins) plopped into the bathtub. Great-Grandma was washing them and scrubbing them real good. "I can't tell if you're clean or not, because the water is so purple,"great-Grandma laughed.

Just then she dropped the soap and began to grope around the mysterious dark waters for it. By now, the bubbles were shrinking and disappearing. The surface was an eerie hue. The

little ones were looking for the soap, too. They laughed and giggled when someone's foot was grabbed instead. All of a sudden, just like a sonar, everyone located the phantom soap at the same time. Voices chimed, "I have it! I have it!"

Four little hands and my great-Grandma's hand plucked out what appeared to be small gray clumps of soap. Great-Grandma let out a loud scream as she flung the clump across the bathroom. Then, the little ones squealed and screamed. Tim yelled really loud, "It's squishy squids!"

With that, everyone jumped out of the bathtub spilling water and squids everywhere! The laughing, screaming, crying and splashing was so loud, great-Grandpa came running. "What's this? Oh, my bee bees. Oh, no! Oh, no!" he stammered as Avalon ran out of the bathroom to hide.

Great-Grandma was laughing so hard, tears ran down her face. There were squids all over the bathroom. Everyone was yelling and laughing except for Avalon, who was nowhere in sight.

A few months later, my great-Grandpa died. He had wanted to live long enough so all of us would remember him, even the babies. We miss him very much. None of us ever take a bath without thinking of him and his birthday squids!

PORK ADOBO

Recipes by Tex Almeria
1 pound pork loin, cut into chunks
1 medium head of garlic, crushed
1/4 cup soy sauce
1/2 cup white vinegar
1 cup water
1 bay leaf
1 teaspooon peppercorn

Place pork in medium-size pot together with the rest of the ingredients. Bring to boil, then simmer for about 45 minutes. Serve hot with rice.

Serves 4.

LUMPIA --FILIPINO EGGROLL

2 tablespoons corn/vegetable oil for sauce
1/2 cup corn/vegetable oil for frying
1 tablespoon minced garlic
1/2 cup chopped onion
3 carrots, diced
1/4 pound fresh string beans diagonally sliced very thin
2 tablespoons soy sauce
1 package lumpia wrappers or eggroll wrappers
1 1/2 cups chicken broth

Heat 2 tablespoons oil in pan. Saute garlic until light brown. Add onion, pork and broth. Simmer for about 20 minutes. Add carrots, string beans and soy sauce. Cook until vegetables are tender. Set aside.

On a flat surface, spread out wrapper. Put 2 tablespoons of filling in each wrapper. Make roll by folding each end of the wrapper to seal in the filling.

Heat 1/2 cup corn/vegetable oil. Deep-fry lumpia on medium heat until brown. Serve hot.

Makes 1 dozen.

GROWING UP IN GLOBEVILLE, COLORADO

Diana Mae Reisbick Shares Reminiscences of Her Early Childhood with Her Volga-German Grandparents

by Carl Ruby

My father, Adam Reisbick, died a month after I was born in 1938. My mother, Mollie, and I went to live with her parents, Elizabeth and Henry Krieger in a place just north of Denver called Globeville. My grandparents were born in Russia, but Grandfather Henry told me they were Volga-Germans. Sometimes he would say it in German, "Die Wolga-Deutschen." He said that a queen called Catherine the Great invited some German people to come to Russia to farm by the Volga River. His grandparents accepted and so did a lot of other German families.

Did I tell you that I was born in Denver, Colorado, United States of America! On May 13 at 13 minutes to 5. I was the 13th baby born that day at the hospital, so 13 has been a special number for me.

Living with immigrant grandparents might sound dull and boring. Not in the Krieger house. My first five years of childhood were filled with a variety of exciting times.

Like every time there was a birth in Globeville, Grandmother Krieger and I would walk two blocks toward the mountains and then two blocks to the left to get to Grandmother Reisbick's house. She's my father's mother. Grandmother Reisbick was a midwife and helped deliver babies right in the home. Within a few seconds she would have her medical-looking black bag in her hand and out the door we went. It was a short parade: First

Grandmother Reisbick, followed by Grandmother Krieger and just a little way back was me, Little Diana, almost in a run trying to keep up with them. Down the street we would march toward the house soon to have an infant. After seeing this parade so many times and each time there was a new baby, the neighborhood kids all thought the new babies came from the black bag. So did I! Grandmother Elizabeth would bring the chicken noodle soup and the rye bread. I just brought myself.

Both my grandmothers believed that chicken noodle soup and rye bread cured everything. If you were sick or tired, out came the soup and bread. Grandfather Henry even credited the bread for his fishing success. His secret was to mix the soft middle of the loaf with cotton and slip that on the hook. Every fish in Colorado loved rye bread. I liked the soup better!

Eating at Grandmother and Grandfather Krieger's was always an adventure because of all the rules we had to follow. No matter what the season, the dining room windows were not to be opened during dinner. I guess this kept the aroma of kraut kuchen — or whatever was being eaten — in the dining room. I didn't mind the smell of kraut kuchen. They are made of cooked cabbage, fried onions and browned, seasoned ground beef baked inside bread dough. It was a sandwich with all the sides closed. In the summertime, the dining room was plain HOT!

The other rule at the dinner table was: NO LAUGHING! If you did you had to leave. Grandpa Henry said that sitting down to nutritious food carefully and lovingly prepared was serious business. You came to the table to eat! It was respectful to talk with a low voice. Laughing was for after the table was cleared. When my mother's brother, Uncle ReDoy came to supper, he made me laugh, so I had to eat my dinner in the kitchen. There, I ate with the window wide open.

On Sundays, other rules were followed. The afternoon lunch was the big meal of the day. Grandpa Henry said that was the way it was since he was a kid. And that's a long time ago! There was no

cooking afterward. In fact, no work was done the rest of the day. Grandpa explained that to me by opening his Bible and reading Exodus 31:15. "Six days may work be done; but in the seventh is the Sabbath of rest, holy to the LORD..." You see, he told me that a lot of Volga-Germans left Russia because they wanted more religious freedoms.

Grandmother Krieger did not allow any smoking, drinking, or card playing in the house. So Grandpa Henry built a garage-like clubhouse for the men. To help decorate the walls, he had me put my bare feet into leftover paint cans, then he lifted me up and I walked over the walls and ceiling. My footprints were everywhere. For days, I was the only girl on the block with painted, pale-blue toenails.

There was also a strict routine for cleaning house. I helped with the ironing on Tuesday. I had a little woodstove-heated iron that I used to press pillowcases and handkerchiefs. During the winter, it was a warming household chore.

I also helped with the dusting on Friday. Even if something

wasn't dusty, you still had to dust it. The things in the dining room were never dusty, because the windows were always closed. That's where I did my best work.

My grandparents had some funny names for food. Hamburger was called "loose meat." Once Grandpa Henry and I found some cooking in the oven. He quickly fried chopped onion and added it to the meat along with salt and pepper. When it was done to his liking, we both sat at the kitchen table and ate it with rye bread. When Grandmother came home, she asked who had seen the horsemeat for the dogs. I was sick immediately.

There were no day-care centers. When my mother was working, Grandmother Elizabeth was my babysitter. When Grandmother went to citizenship school, I went with her. I was the only child in the class! When Grandmother quilted with the older women, I went with her. My stitches were too big, so I threaded their needles. When Grandmother attended every Globeville funeral, I went with her. I even had a special black coat and little black hat. I was her trailer. She towed me everywhere.

Grandmother Krieger knew just about every Volga-German in Globeville. Most of them were from the same Russian town of Norka where she once lived. All those families that immigrated had to have a United States sponsor, someone who would make sure they would have a job and a place to stay. So why do they all live in Globeville? A "Mr. Wolfe" was everyone's sponsor and he lived here.

When I played next door, I usually took the shortcut through a hole in the hedge. One day, I was called home, but for some reason I took the long way around to the front of the house. As I walked under the tree in the front yard, something hit me in the head. Buster, our dog, barked and growled. People screamed and yelled. A porcupine had jumped or fallen from the tree on me. Buster had to go to the animal doctor to get the quills removed. I got the universal Globeville medication, Unguentine. Unguentine was a thick ointment or salve made of eucalyptus and thyme oils that healed and soothed. Its odor is hard to explain, sort of a medicinal, hospital smell mixed with lime Kool-Aid. Nothing quite has the scent of Unguentine, but everyone in Globeville knew its distinct aroma. I smelled like Unguentine for weeks.

Once, I sneaked some chocolate from the store across the street. I ate it in small pieces. The name on the wrapper was Ex-lax.

Grandmother Krieger had storage bins built into the pantry that held all the different flours for all the bread she made. Each bin held 50 to 100 pounds of flour and she measured it with a scoop that hung on a hook. One day, there was a mouse in the house. Grandmother chased it. The frightened mouse went into the white-flour bin. Tootsie, our other dog, was called to rid the bin of the mouse. Flour flew everywhere. The dog and everything in the pantry were white as ghosts. The white flour was ruined. The rye flour was saved. I don't know what happened to the mouse. I only know we had everything made with rye flour for many weeks.

My mother had the best job ever! She worked at the soda fountain in the downtown Daniels and Fisher Department Store. Together, she and I invented different sodas. Oh, we made cherry and chocolate Cokes, root beer floats and all the flavored sodas with vanilla ice cream. But I was adventurous and made chocolate sodas with strawberry ice cream, a double chocolate-chocolate, and once I went down the syrup line and put in a squirt of each flavor. There was chocolate, butterscotch, strawberry, cherry, pineapple and maybe a few more all in one soda. Even though it looked like mud, it tasted okay. Of all the ones we concocted, my favorite was a pineapple with chocolate ice cream. I always drank my soda served with a white cupcake.

Growing up in Globeville, Colorado, with my Mom and her parents, was filled with adventure and excitement every minute of the day, every day. I only wish my Dad could have been there.

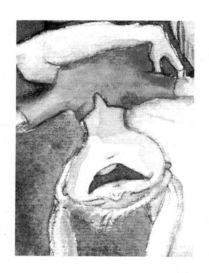

GRANDMOTHER KRIEGER'S RYE BREAD

DAY ONE

3 cups light rye flour
1 package (1/4 ounce) dry yeast
3 1/2 cups water

Mix all ingredients to make a sticky dough. Cover and let sit overnight.

NEXT DAY

Preheat oven to 400°F
4 cups white flour

Add the 4 cups white flour to the overnight mixture. Mix well. Cover with a wet cloth and place in a warm place to rise.

Grease and flour three 9" x 5" loaf pans. Fill each pan half full with dough. Let sit about 30 minutes in a warm place. Sprinkle with water and place in the hot 400°F oven for 15 minutes. Reduce oven temperature to 350° for 35 to 40 minutes or until the bread is golden brown.

Makes 3 loaves.

Seder Surprise

Barbara Winerich-Cantwell Recalls a Passover Dinner
with Her Grandmother

by Renee Fajardo

For Jewish people, Passover is a very sacred time. It occurs in springtime and represents the end of slavery and the preciousness of freedom. In ancient times, when the people were slaves in Egypt, they had a chance to be free and had to escape very quickly. When they left, there was no time to let their bread rise, so they had to take the unbaked dough with them. Later, when they baked it, it was thin and crispy. This unleavened bread was called matzo. From this ancient beginning, matzo became one of the most important foods in all our Sabbaths and festivals. It is the focal point of the ritual dinner ceremony called Seder on the first night of Passover.

As a little girl, I attended Seders at my grandmother's house. Booboo Bell, as we called her, lived in a very old part of downtown Denver in a second-story apartment. My grandfather died long before I was born and, in order to support herself and her children, Booboo Bell sold second-hand clothes. Everyone in the neighborhood knew her and respected her for her business sense as well as her ability to make the best out of a bad situation. When her children grew up, Booboo Bell continued to collect and repair second-hand clothes.

This worked out well for all of us grandchildren, because every year before Passover, she gave us all near-new outfits. This was the signal that the time to prepare for the Seder was upon us. Shortly afterward, the real work began. Booboo Bell's apartment

was cleaned from top to bottom. All the linen was laundered, walls were scrubbed and windows were washed. The Passover dishes were unpacked, the silverware and the pots were koshered by boiling them and all the hamatez, the leavened bread, was removed from the apartment or burned. Special foods were bought and we made haroset, an apple, cinnamon, nut and wine mixture. All this preparation made the anticipation of Seder so much more exciting!

One Seder in particular sticks out in my mind. I was only ten years old and all my cousins, aunts and uncles were at Booboo Bell's. Uncle Jacob poured the first cup of wine for all of us, then he filled the Elijah cup for the great prophet who is said to have ridden to Heaven in a fiery chariot and who will return to announce the Messiah. The cup is set to welcome his return.

The Uncle Jacob said kiddush — a prayer — over the wine. This begins the Seder service.

The Seder plate contains all the special foods. There is horseradish to remind us of the bitter life our people had in Egypt. There is a meat bone and a hard-boiled egg representing the Passover offering, salt water representing tears shed by the people, karpas, vegetables to represent Spring, fruitfulness and hope. There is also haroset, which signifies the clay used by the slaves to make bricks. There are three cakes of matzo covered on a separate plate. These cakes of matzo represented the haste with which the Jewish people left Egypt to find freedom.

One of the cakes is broken in half, wrapped and placed

under the table cloth. This, of course, was a traditional part of the Seder. The afikomen, the broken cakes, are to be eaten by everyone after they are finished with dinner. It is the last piece of the meal. Sometimes, one of us children would steal the afikomen and Uncle Jacob offered a reward for its return.

On this particular Seder, Cousin BJ did the honor of "stealing" the afikomen. I saw him put it in his coat pocket during the main dinner. He thought no one noticed and could hardly contain his smirk throughout the meal. He was thinking about the reward Uncle Jacob would offer. Small coins and pieces of candy or maybe even something more tantalizing like real paper money!

When the meal was finally finished, Uncle Jacob began to look for the afikomen. He acted surprised when he couldn't find it. Then he offered a reward for its return. Every child giggled. Cousin BJ was so excited, he jumped up from the table and shouted, "It's in my overcoat pocket, Booboo Bell!"

The rest of us laughed at him. He didn't have a clue how to build the excitement level. Oh well, there was always next year and someone more devilish could steal it then.

"Oy vey," Booboo Bell exclaimed, "BJ, the matzo isn't wrapped up. Look at this dirty pocket," she held up a napkin accusingly.

Then she pulled out the matzo. "And someone has been noshing on it!"

Now BJ had everyone's attention. Playing the game was one thing, eating the matzo before the end of dinner was another thing.

"I didn't eat on it!" BJ protested.

Booboo Bell reached into the pocket again and pulled out something else. That something squirmed and jiggled.

"A mouse in my house?" she demanded.

The table hummed in protest. Small shrieks and gagging sounds followed by directions for the creature's disposal.

"Throw it in the trash."

"Hush it."

"Stuff it in a plastic bag."

"Filthy thing. Kill it."

"Smash it in the head."

"I found it in Uncle Sal's store cellar, Booboo Bell. I just wanted a pet. I thought he was in the other pocket," BJ said sadly.

"Well, this is a fine mess, BJ! What am supposed to do with this mouse, eh?" Booboo Bell asked. "Do you have a suggestion, Barbara?" She glanced at me.

I usually don't talk too much. Maybe that's why she asked me. I was the only one not yelling at the time. "I don't know. It's Passover. I guess we should set it free," I said.

"Good answer, shayna punim — pretty face. Sal, take the mouse downstairs and let it go. Jacob, use another one of the matzo cakes for the afikomen. Everyone close your mouths and mind your own business. Mr. BJ, creatures need to be free, not little boys' pets."

With that order, the Seder continued until late at night. We read, sang and prayed. When it was time to go home, Booboo Bell kissed me on the forehead and said, "Freedom is a very tiring job."

I never forgot that Seder nor how a matzo cake and a mouse came to symbolize that freedom is basic to all beings.

Matzo Balls for Chicken Soup

Evie Hudak's Passover Recipes

6 tablespoons fat or oil
4 eggs
1 cup matzo meal
4 tablespoons chicken soup broth
1/2 teaspoon salt

In a mixing bowl, mix together the fat or oil with the eggs and salt. Then mix in the matzo meal. (For harder balls, add 1 or 2 more tablespoons of matzo meal; for softer balls, add 1 more tablespoon of soup.)

Cover the mixing bowl and place in the refrigerator for at least 20 minutes.

Using a 2- or 3-quart pot, bring salted water to a brisk boil. Reduce the heat, and slowly drop in balls of the matzo meal mixture (about 3/4-inch in diameter). Cover the pot and cook for 30-40 minutes.

Strain the balls out of the cooking water, and put them into a large pot of soup.

Simmer the matzo balls in the soup for several minutes before serving.

Haroset — Apple-nut Mixture for the Seder

6 Red Delicious apples
1-1/2 cups walnuts, finely chopped
3 teaspoons cinnamon
3 teaspoons sugar
6 tablespoons sweet concord grape wine (or non-alcoholic sweet red wine)

Peel and core the apples. Grate them coarsely. Mix in the chopped nuts, then the cinnamon, sugar and, finally, the wine. Put in an air-tight container and chill.

Serve as a relish or as a topping on matzo.

christmas Day in Jamaica

Delores Came from Jamaica to New York in 1950 and Now Lives in Colorado.

by Carl Ruby

The sun shines on Jamaica at Christmas time. All across the vast city of Kingston, the food for Christmas Day is plentiful and carefully prepared according to family customs. Jamaican culture is shaped by many influences: West African, Spanish and English. The cuisine has an African flavor influenced by Europe, Asia and North America. There are no public decorations – the bounty and beauty of the country are sufficient ornament.

In the suburb of Franklintown, just past South Camp Road, 9-year-old Delores and her grandmother make ready the dishes for Christmas Day. It is everyday fare that takes on a festive, ceremonial flair: Chicken, rice and peas, as well as the Christmas cake. A string of colored lights hangs in the living room over the door to the kitchen. The lights are a gift from Uncle, who bought them in the United States.

The chicken, fresh from Grandmother's flock, waits in the refrigerator, seasoned with salt, black pepper and ginger, along with sliced onions. It will be fricasseed, for the early Christmas afternoon dinner.

Rice and beans, staples of the Jamaican diet, start with coconuts, cut open, the water drained. The white coconut "meat" is shredded and warm water added. Grandmother squeezes the juice with her hands, while Delores picks over and washes the dry red beans.

Kidney or goongo (pigeon) beans are cooked with the liquid and are done when they mash between your fingers. Thyme, salt, pepper, onions and green scallions are added. The juice is used to cook the rice. When the rice is done, the beans go in.

Jamaican Christmas cake originates from the traditional English plum pudding. It is full of fruit soaked in wine and rum. The cake is prepared months beforehand so that it can be doused frequently to preserve its gummy consistency.

Delores wakes Christmas morning and looks into her stocking, just a regular sock. She takes it down from the tall post on the corner of her iron bed and finds a whistle, a horn, a pack of clappers and a small doll. The apple comes from the States. But Santa forgot the brightly painted tin tea set.

"What happened to Santa?" Delores asks.

"He'll come later on," her auntie replies. She has arrived early to help with the morning chores and attend church with Grandmother and Delores.

"I met him on the street and he said he was afraid the tin would make a hole in your stocking," Grandmother adds.

The Christmas market in Victoria Park on King's Street downtown is decorated with colorful stalls waiting for the after-church crowd to gather and buy last minute toys, firecrackers and sparklers. Balloons of every color float everywhere. Clappers and starlights add to the sounds of happy laughter. Everyone's in a festive mood when Delores and Grandmother arrive. They have attended early morning church services dressed in their Sunday, colorful best and now will stay at the park until 10 o'clock, then take the tram car home. Grandmother makes a secret purchase, while Delores observes the crowd mingling on such a peaceful Jamaican morning.

Rover greets Grandmother and Delores. Delores pets the white dog and scratches his one brown ear. Grandmother disappears and soon reappears from Delore's bedroom saying, "I think Santa left something on the top of the wardrobe. We must

have missed it when we were hurrying to get to early morning services."

It's the tin tea set! Just the perfect blue color she wanted.

After the traditional fricasseed chicken dinner, Delores and her grandmother attend the Ward Theatre's live stage show. This year, the play features native music and dancing. It's a marvelous gathering and after the show, everyone hurries home to host friends who'll soon be dropping by to share and sample this year's Christmas cake. Delores hopes she'll find the six pence coin Grandmother has baked inside. Other people include silver hearts or rings or a rooster's wishbone in their cakes. The buried surprises are symbols on which the finder's future will be decided.

The next day is Boxing Day, another public holiday that's a holdover from British rule, when gifts were traditionally given to service workers. Delores and her grandmother don't celebrate Boxing Day. They will still have friends and family dropping by, and, of course, Delores will be playing with her new blue tin tea set. To the common people of Jamaica, Boxing Day is just one extra day of Christmas.

As the sun sets on the City of Kingston, one Christmas Day has ended. Delores is tucked into her bed anticipating another Christmas Day, tomorrow. Sweet dreams, Delores!

Jamaican Fricasseed Chicken

1 chicken (4 to 6 pounds, quartered)

1/8 teaspoon black pepper

1/4 teaspoon salt

1/2 teaspoon ginger

3 large onion, one sliced, two coarsely chopped

1/4 cup oil

3 medium tomatoes, coarsely chopped

1 clove garlic, chopped

1 whole and unbroken green Scotch bonnet or chili pepper

1/2 teaspoon paprika

2 tablespoons hot water

1 tablespoon butter, melted

1 tablespoon Worcestershire sauce

Wash and thoroughly dry chicken and season with black pepper, salt, ginger and sliced onion. Leave covered overnight in refrigerator. Next day, remove the onions and pat the chicken dry. Cut chicken into smaller pieces. Brown on all sides in hot oil. Lower heat and add tomatoes, garlic, unbroken green pepper, chopped onion, paprika and hot water. Cover and simmer, adding small amounts of hot water as necessary. Chicken should be fork tender when cooked. Add melted butter and Worcestershire sauce just before serving.

Serves 4 to 6 people.

Karina's Story

*Karina Revisits Her Navajo Family for Her Niece's
Kinaalda Ceremony*

by Renee Fajardo

Karina hadn't been down
Gulch Mine Road for almost 10 years. She had made the 500-mile
trek from Colorado to Farmington once a year for the last few
years out of obligation to her grandmother who had moved into
town after her grandfather died. Occasionally, during Karina's
week-long visit, her grandma mentioned going up to the land.
Perhaps hinting that Karina should go back just to visit. Somehow,
the 40-mile trip seemed like 400, so she never went.

Now, here she was, against her better judgment, driving the
worst stretch of dirt road in all of New Mexico. Times change, but
this road hadn't. It was as bumpy, dusty and narrow as it had
always been. She wondered how her grandmother faired on the
trip earlier that morning. She'd probably driven with Uncle Joe in
his ancient pick-up truck. Karina smiled thinking about how that
truck must have rattled going down the road. "Just like popping
corn," Uncle Joe always said.

Most of the relatives were already at Grandmother's land.
Some of the aunts had been at the hogan since yesterday,
preparing for the ceremony. Tonight and tomorrow, the rest of the
relatives would come. Since Grandmother was getting on in years,
she insisted that everyone attend Belinda's kinaalda. Even Karina
couldn't refuse. She didn't really see the point of having the

ceremony. In fact, the last one she'd attended had been her own. The thought struck her by surprise. That was the last time she had traveled Gulch Mine Road, going to her own kinaalda! She even recalled thinking, back then, that she never wanted to go to one again.

Karina's own kinaalda distressed her. Although it was a Navajo custom and a great honor, she had been a shy 13 year old. She had her first moon while she was away at boarding school. Her grandmother and aunt were so excited about her initiation to womanhood, they had pulled her out of school mid-week. Of course, everyone at school knew she'd started menstruating and was off to her kinaalda ceremony. Karina just wanted to fit in, not to have a bunch of attention drawn to her.

There was, of course, the long drive from school to Grandmother's land. Down the dusty, bumpy, narrow Gulch Mine Road. When she finally arrived at Grandmother's hogan, there were dozens of relatives already there. Some were digging the hole for the kinaalda cake; some were butchering sheep for stew; some were cleaning the hogan; others piled that mountain of corn Karina was going to have to grind by hand.

She was led into a small hogan, where her grandmother and aunt brushed her hair with a grass bush and braided white yarn into it. Then the singing of the prayers began and Karina was presented with her kinaalda outfit. A beautiful, purple, velvet skirt and traditional Navajo white, billowing blouse. Her belt was a red, hand-woven sash made by her aunt. And, of course, there was the marvelous family turquoise jewelry.

At the instruction of the medicine man, Karina was molded by her aunt. This is what the original Holy People did to Changing Women. They molded her, so she could mold others and her children, someday. Karina still remembered the long line of people at the hogan door awaiting her healing magic touch. It seemed to take forever to mold the 60-some people that had come.

After the molding, she started her run. Her kinaalda lasted four days, with daily runs in early morning and afternoon. She ran toward the East, the beginning of the day, and the people she had molded followed her. Each day she ran farther than the day before. She remembered corn pollen being put on her head and lips. This was to help her follow the Sacred Road.

After the run, Karina returned to the hogan to begin the long, hard chore of preparing her cake. This meant grinding corn by hand all day long! The men prepared an oven in the ground by digging a 4-foot wide hole. On the last day of the ceremony, a big fire would be started in the hole to heat the earth. That is also when the kinaalda cake batter would be prepared.

She had also sewed corn husk for hours. These were made into a sort of round blanket that would be used to protect the crust of the cake. It was almost as tedious as grinding corn for hours! But it was necessary so that the batter of corn meal, sprouted wheat and brown sugar could be poured into the hole over the corn-husk blanket. Then, another layer of corn-husk blanket was placed on top of the batter. Wet newspapers were placed on top of the corn husk and, after that, a layer of dirt was spread over the hole. This order of things ensured a properly cooked cake. Finally, the fire was started over the top of the hole and the cake was allowed to bake all night.

Karina winced at the memory of what followed. All night long she had to sit straight-legged and pray. The medicine man started the singing and the others joined in. This went on for hours and hours until sunrise. At sunrise, she could begin another run. The last run was followed by one more molding and then the beautiful cake was unearthed and served to all the guests. The medicine man and her grandmother received the center pieces for being very special guests.

Such an ancient ceremony, Karina thought to herself. Why didn't she feel more affectionate about her own kinaalda? Navajo by birth but living in a world that was not Navajo. The memories of her childhood and the realities of the big city did not fit. Karina sometimes forgot she was Diné when she was working at her computer job. She felt just like everyone else. She worked five days a week, 9 to 5, paid bills and took night classes at the local college. She'd become almost convinced that the ceremonies of her youth were the dreams of the old people, repeated in the hopes that someone would remember, but in the end were doomed to be forgotten.

Karina glanced at the horizon and stared in bleak recognition. There before her were the teepee mounds. The distant piles of earth looked strange on the otherwise flat plains. These mounds were the tailings left from the mines, when the bulldozers dug the coal out of the earth. They looked ghostly.

Glancing in her rear view mirror, Karina saw there were no herds of sheep grazing the land. In her youth, the high plain stretching before her was covered with a tendril green fuzz. The land was vibrant with life and everywhere you looked there were small clusters of black and white sheep.

Things change. The power plant that burned the coal had been polluting this area for years. The terrible cough and breathing problems of the old ones were the first signs of this pollution. And now the land lay brown and dead. Only the power plant remained.

Suddenly, Karina felt a rush of adrenaline. She let her foot off the gas petal and braked slightly. She bounced in her seat. Her heart beat against her chest. She laughed to herself. It was Hoss Ridge. The granddaddy of all potholes. And it was still as deep as it had always been.

The appearance of Hoss Ridge meant Old Man White's hogan was only a few hundred yards away. She couldn't recollect why John White was called Old Man. It probably had something to do with the fact that his long, braided hair had been snow-white for a long as anyone could remember. Karina's grandmother said it was because he was very wise and had endured so much sorrow in his life without becoming bitter or angry.

Old Man White had a couple of sons, but they were teenagers and on their own by the time Karina had come to know the family. There had been some kind of fight between them and they didn't talk to each other. The youngest child, Rosa, was Old Man White's only daughter. Rosa and Karina played together every summer. Rosa didn't go to school. She was taught reading and writing at home. She herded sheep, collected herbs and sang prayers. Rosa was gifted with the Sight and her dad didn't want it causing problems for Rosa at school. She saw all kinds of things: like storms coming, the sex of babies, accidents about to occur ... A gift like that can be a big burden when you're only a kid. Sometimes John White couldn't tell if people were visiting to be sociable or just to ask Rosa a question.

Karina and Rosa were like sisters. They sat on the hood of John White's truck all night long and stared at the stars. What they talked about, Karina couldn't recall.

The memory of Rosa was unbearably painful. Karina realized that she hadn't traveled this road from the time she was 13. All these years she'd believed it was because she'd disliked her kinaalda so much. But, really, it wasn't so bad. Rosa had been there, helping the aunts prepare for it.

She was proud of Karina and almost more excited than Karina's grandmother. Karina insisted that Rosa's kinaalda would be just as nice, but Rosa had said she wouldn't be having one. Karina laughed. If anyone would have a kinaalda, it would be

Rosa, brought up in the old ways. But Rosa was right.

On the way home from visiting her aunt, Rosa died in a car crash. Karina never got to say good-bye. The old ways, the Sight, the prayers had done no good to protect her friend.

She still felt the bitterness of her loss. She hadn't gone to Rosa's funeral. She never visited John White either. Her anger settled into a dark place at the back of her mind and stayed there, taking up such a little space, it was barely noticed.

When Karina was 15, after her family moved to town, she ran into John White in the hardware store. He saw her across the street and waved her over. Tears welled in Karina's eyes remembering the meeting. John White told her he understood why she hadn't been around for so long. He told her sometimes death comes too young. He said the Great Spirit is not for us to question. Things are taken away. Things are given. He said he had a gift for her the next time she came by. But she never went. She moved to Colorado and tried to forget.

A loud popping jerked Karina back to the present. A sickening "ka-thud, ka-thud." She pulled the car over. Great time to get a flat and no way to fix it. She locked the car and started walking.

Old Man White's hogan was just ahead. Maybe he still lived there. She walked up to the door and was about to knock when she heard the familiar Gulch Mine cough behind her. Karina jumped and jerked around. "Oh," she stammered. "I'm Karina."

"I haven't seen you for 10 years, child," a familiar voice said.

"I'm 25 years old now," Karina said almost defiantly.

Old Man White hardly looked a day older. He wore the same tan pants and plaid shirt she remembered from the last time she saw him.

"I mean, I'm surprised you recognized me. It's been a long time," she said, but he seemed to look past her straight into the mid-day sun.

"Yes," he said flatly. "Come inside. You can have a cup of

cool water."

Karina nodded, unsmiling for fear she might offend him. "Sure," she said, "water sounds nice." She hoped he had a truck to take her the rest of the way to Grandmother's land.

He waved her into the hogan. She pushed open the door and hesitated a moment while her eyes adjusted to the light. It was much as she recalled. Clean and neat, filled with family pictures. A small wooden table and two cots. The water jug stood on the counter by the sink. Two cups lay beside it, almost as if John White had been expecting company. Two bowls with spoons and a basket of fry bread sat on the table. There was a small pan, cold on the stove, filled with mutton, seasoned with sage.

Old Man White looked at Karina. His dark eyes were cloudy with cataracts.

"Would you like something to eat?" he asked gently.

"Of course," Karina said, obligingly. "I'll serve the food. Please sit. It was very nice of you to ask me in."

She poured two cups of water, filled the bowls with the meat and sat down across from John White.

"Were you expecting company?" she asked.

"No. I was just waiting." He ate a small bite of mutton and tore a piece of fry bread.

"You know, my boys live about 15 miles east of here. They're both married and have three children each. They live almost next door to each other. One works at the power plant. He's an environmental engineer trying to figure out how to clean up this place." Old Man White laughed. "The other one is a teacher. They get along just fine. When Rosa passed away, they mended their differences. The Great Spirit works in funny ways sometimes."

The mention of Rosa made Karina squirm. "I'm sorry..." she began.

"No, no. No need to be sorry. It's been a long time. It's time for Rosa to rest now."

Karina ate and drank the water, grateful for something to occupy her mouth other than words.

Finally, she said, "I loved coming here when I was child."

"You were always welcome. Rosa loved you. I have the gift I told you I'd give you if you ever came by. Climb up to the shelf over there and look in that little box on the top."

Karina did as she was told and placed the box on the table.

"Open it up. Food for the soul," John smiled.

There was the turquoise necklace Rosa had worn all her life. The loveliest color of green-blue Karina had ever seen. The single stone was shaped like an ear of corn and lay inside two silver husks.

"I don't know what to say. I can't believe you've held on to this for so long."

"I told you. I've been waiting."

Karina placed the necklace around her neck.

"I don't have a truck," he said. "But if you go now and run hard for a quarter mile up the road, you'll catch the tail end of the Kinaalda runners. You can take your time then and run to your grandmother's hogan. Someone there is bound to have a truck." He laughed. "Better go now!"

Karina stood and thanked him. Outside, she began to run.

"What's going on?" she thought as her legs picked up speed. The faster she ran, the more Rosa's necklace swayed and thumped against her chest and across her shoulders. Her heart pounded. As long as she was running, the moment seemed eternal. She realized that all she had to do to stop running was remove the necklace. But even if she wanted to, her body could not.

The rhythm of her heart and the sound of her feet striking the ground were almost musical. Sweat dripped down her forehead. The wind whistled past her ears. The heat of the sun drew into her bones. The air vibrated. The necklace pelted her as if to pound out the hidden secrets of her own body. Up ahead,

she saw small outlines of other people running, following a girl in a long dress. The kinaalda runners. Karina's heart beat wildly and joyfully. Soon she'd be a part of their rhythm. She ran faster. Faster than she'd ever run.

She was sweating by the time she caught up. People laughed and slapped her back. The necklace bobbed as she slowed her pace to an easy trot. The remaining four miles were calm and tranquil. She listened to the sounds of runners and smelled the sage. The whole earth was alive to her. She thought of dear, sweet Rosa. She imagined her grandmother's surprised face. She hummed old songs she thought she'd forgotten. She tasted the sweat salt on her lips. She breathed so deep, she took in the universe. Suddenly, all those childhood conversations with Rosa came back to her.

"Karina!" Grandmother shouted as she approached the hogan. "Oh my! You ran with the runners. How?"

Karina was breathless and her voice barely audible. "Old Man White..." she whispered.

Grandmother's eyes widened. "You are full of surprises today. How did you hear John White had passed on?"

Karina's ears rang. "What? When?"

"Last week. About noon, on Monday. His boys were with him. He'd been sick a long time, but he had a peaceful passing."

Tears poured down Karina's face. She sat on the ground and sobbed uncontrollably. She clutched the necklace with one hand and Grandmother's skirt hem with the other. She remembered so much, suddenly. Things changed like needles on a pine tree in Spring. But the roots remained firmly planted in the rich, dark earth. She was Diné. She had always been Diné, she always would. And as her tears fell, she remembered more than she knew.

Fry Bread

Recipes by Josephine Petterson

Note: Adult supervision is required.

2 cups all-purpose flour
cup powdered milk
teaspoon salt
3/4 teaspoon baking powder
1/8 cup shortening
cup cold water
vegetable oil for frying

Mix all dry ingredients. Make a hole in the middle. Add shortening and water. Knead with your hands until all the shortening is combined with the flour mixture.

Knead in the rest of the ingredients. Add more flour or water if needed, small amounts at a time, enough to make a soft, workable ball of dough. Let rise for an hour.

About 15 minutes before the hour is up, fill a deep skillet or Dutch oven or fry daddy more than halfway with vegetable oil. Heat until hot but not smoking, to about 350°

Punch down and knead into a ball again. Make small balls. Then roll them into round circles about 1/8-inch thick. Make a little hole in each circle with the middle of your finger.

Deep fry in hot oil about 2 minutes on both sides or until fry bread is golden brown.

Drain fry bread on a platter layered with paper towels to soak excess oil.

Often served with honey or powdered sugar or as Navajo tacos.
Makes 1 dozen.

Navajo Tacos

1 dozen fry breads

1 pound cooked hamburger meat

1 can pinto beans

1 cup shredded cheese

2 cups shredded lettuce

1 cup chopped tomatoes

cup minced onions

Place ingredients in separate bowls. Garnish fry bread with beans, meat, lettuce, tomatoes, onions, and top with cheese. You may also add salsa to taste.

A Letter to Sister Alyce

While Stationed in Germany During the Korean War, Japanese-American Sergeant Shozo Watanabe Writes to His Older Sister His Thoughts About Their Family's Internment by the United States Government During World War II

by Carl Ruby

Dear Alyce,

It's getting close to the holidays, so I thought I would write you. I'm in the barracks. I just got off a communication watch. The Air Force has Staff Sergeant Watanabe on duty for New Year's Eve. Sometimes on these watches your mind wanders. Just today I was thinking back to when I was 10.

You must remember Lathrop, California. The rented house between the railroad tracks was a great place. The "jungle" space filled with trees and bushes by the tracks was a wondrous spot for us nine kids to play. It was exciting when we found gypsies camped there. The orchard on the other side of the house provided many hours of work and tree climbing. Who was it that fell and broke an arm?

The house was a plain, brownish two-story with the stairs to the second floor on the outside. I thought that was odd, but not as weird as having the water tank above the house!

Mama always had something cooking on the wood-burning stove. I think I can smell the rice cooking now! I can see the long, rectangular kitchen table down the middle of the room. Papa always sat at the head. We kids sat anywhere we liked.

It was Frank who helped smash the rice for the New Year's mochi. The hollow tree stump in the orchard made the perfect "bowl" for crushing the cooked rice. I think Papa put a big pot or something inside the trunk before the pounding started. Frank looked important with the long wooden sticks. The rice was given to Mama and she finished the mochi by adding beans to the middle of each rice lump. She made them every New Year. I know, I ate my fill many times over.

That 1942 New Year's celebration was the last our family had in that house. December 7, 1941 changed our lives. Pearl Harbor. Papa was born in Japan, but at the age of 18, he ventured to Hawai'i, joined the U.S. Army during World War I and, after the war, married Mama, who was a native Hawai'ian. They moved to California, found work and started to raise a family. Both became United States citizens. Then they received the letter that said they must leave California by April 1942. Papa told me that an Army general said, "Once a Jap, always a Jap." We had to move and I was mad. I didn't want to leave our home, my school and all my friends. I wanted to stay exactly where we were.

I know you remember the next months. You helped me pack my suitcase with a few clothes and my bedding. You were instructed not to pack any Oriental or Japanese things. Papa gave those away! He didn't want strangers to have our belongings. A bus came for us. They looked through our suitcases and bedding. Lily had to give up her favorite Japanese doll. They drove us to the Stockton Race Track. The armed guards called it the Assembly Center. The barns and horse stalls became our home. I didn't get used to the smell, did you? Mama no longer cooked. We ate in the mess hall. We had lots of rice and vegetables. The meat we ate had a different taste. Did you ever wonder where all the horses went?

The four months at Stockton seemed forever while we waited around for transportation to a War Relocation Center in Arkansas. Then one day we boarded a train and left California. The

journey took three days. Ken and Bob hated the rocking, confining train. The guards told us to pull down the shades when the train went through a city. Papa said we were wise to keep the shades down, because there were some mad people who would shoot at us because we were Japanese. I was born in the United States, just like you. I will never forget when we got to Rohwer War Relocation Authority Center. You held my hand and Helen's as we left the train car. I was so afraid. The camp was surrounded by a high wire fence with eight guard towers. I could see the guns. Could you? Our new "home" was a rectangular barracks covered all over in black roofing paper. All around us we could hear soldiers shouting orders and Jeep motors racing. How did we ever get through three and half years there? We never seem to talk about that time. I think about it more now that I'm in the Air Force.

I remember that each building had six rooms labeled "A," "B", "C", "D," "E" and "F." Papa and Mama had the "A" room with baby Betty Lou and newborn Ronnie. He was born in the camp, right? You, Lily, Helen and Rose had the "B" room and we guys had the "C." I could never sleep on the top bunk. I think we were in a block of ten barracks. I didn't like eating in the mess hall. I knew that Papa was a camp cook. He was a cook when he was in the U.S. Army. He got paid $16 a month for cooking in the camp. He never ate with us at the long tables.

Just before New Year's, several of the elders went to the mess hall and made the traditional mochi. Frank was not there to smash the rice for them. He was drafted and joined the U.S. Army right there at the camp. Besides New Year's, the other celebrations I remember were the weddings with Mama helping. Those were the few times we had some fun.

Remember that one guard? The one we waited for? I forget his name. We kids would sneak out of the camp and go swimming in the stream in the nearby forest. The guard would say, "I see you! I won't say anything! Get back before I get off duty." You would reply, "Want to go swimming with us?"

Oh, school was school. There were white teachers and Japanese teachers. Only English was spoken. I was in junior high and do you recall how proud Papa and Mama were when I became the school's newspaper editor? What grade were you in?

August 23, 1945! What a day of total excitement. FREE! FREE! FREEDOM! You know that day is forever emblazoned in my brain. At day's end, Papa and Mama gathered us and told us we were leaving. The United States government gave each family money to get back home. The Watanabes had no home. Papa heard that Governor Carr of Colorado had invited the Japanese to live in his state. Papa had a Japanese friend in Fort Lupton, Colorado, and away we went on the train. Ken and Bob didn't mind that ride with the window shades wide open.

As I write this letter, I have many mixed emotions. All I wanted to do is wish you a happy New Year and, instead, you get my version of our family's internment during World War II. Do I resent our government for those years in the camp? I guess I'm still looking for that answer, and I have wondered why we never talk about that time with each other. You are my big sister and I needed you so much during that time. Thank you for listening, Alyce, I just needed someone to let my mind and thoughts ramble. Oh, how I wish I had some mochi!

Your loving brother,
Shozo

Japanese Mochi

BEAN FILLING (make first)

1 pound azuki beans (from any Asian food store)
3 cups sugar
pinch of salt

Wash azuki beans three times and soak overnight.

Next day add the beans to a pan and fill to cover the beans with cold water. Bring to a boil and rinse. Do this three times to remove the bitter taste of the beans. Always start with cold water.

Add the beans to a crock pot, add enough water to cover, and cook all night or until the beans are very soft. Place beans in a clean cloth and squeeze out the water until almost dry. Remove from cloth.

Put beans in a pan and add the sugar and salt and mix. The mixture will be watery. Cook on medium heat for 45 minutes to one hour, stirring constantly with a wood spoon. To test for right consistency, draw spoon across pan: if bean mixture does not come together, cook another 5 minutes. If mixture is too runny, keeping cooking and testing.

Cool and form into little balls. Makes 30 to 35 bean balls. May be frozen if not used right away. Set aside and make dough.

DOUGH

1 box (16 ounce size) mochiko flour (sweet rice flour)
1 1/2cups sugar
2 1/2 cups water

Mix sugar and water until sugar is dissolved: add mochiko and mix.

Line a steamer with screen insert and clean cloth, pour in mixture and steam for 35 minutes. Dough is done when an inserted wooden stick (chopstick) comes out clean.

Pour dough into a bowl and "pound" with a wooden mallet for 2 to 3 minutes. Put dough onto a large piece of foil covered with corn starch. Pinch off a small piece of dough, flatten and add one bean ball to the center, bring dough over the ball and pinch loose ends together. Use small amount of corn starch to keep dough from sticking to fingers when forming mochi. Keep unpinched dough covered with a cloth as dough needs to be kept warm for easy handling. Makes 35 mochi.

My Story

MY PICTURE

My Recipe